Jennifer Jackson
Beth Lefgren

Illustrated by
Jeni Brinton Gochnour

Bookcraft
Salt Lake City, Utah

To all the wonderful people at Bookcraft
for their help and patience.

Copyright © 1997 by Beth Lefgren and Jennifer Jackson

All rights reserved. No part of this book may be reproduced in any form or by any means without permission in writing from the publisher, Bookcraft, Inc., 1848 West 2300 South, Salt Lake City, Utah 84119.

Bookcraft is a registered trademark of Bookcraft, Inc.

Library of Congress Catalog Card Number: 97-74878
ISBN 1-57008-334-7

First Printing, 1997

Printed in the United States of America

Contents

Arts and Crafts

Education and Scholarship

Family History

Family Skills

Health and Personal Grooming

Hospitality

Outdoor Fun and Skills

Personal Preparedness

Safety and Emergency Preparedness

Service and Citizenship

Spirituality

Sports and Physical Fitness

Preface

We are so grateful to have another opportunity to share activity ideas for achievement days. Activities do provide unlimited opportunities to strengthen and teach the young people around us. The right activities can supply a great deal of fun in a gospel-oriented atmosphere. What better way to reach each child than through wholesome, enjoyable activities!

Even though this book was written and formatted for achievement days, we found that many of these activities work well for family home evening and Young Women/Young Men activities. Your own personal creativity and knowledge of the age group with whom you are working can easily adapt most of these ideas to other programs.

In writing this book, we also tried to stay away from time-consuming preparation and costly materials, allowing you to focus on the children in your stewardship. In addition, every activity we have included has been tried (and approved) by children.

We wish you well in whatever capacity you will be using this book. We know that you will find great blessings in working with these young brothers and sisters, and we hope that this book will help you achieve the best possible program.

How to Use This Book

This book contains a wide variety of activities. We have endeavored to offer a large selection so you can choose the best one to meet your specific needs. To help you use these activities, you might apply the following suggestions:

1. Notice that the activities are grouped into the twelve areas of achievement as outlined in the achievement days program. However, most activities can easily be adjusted to meet goals in Young Women, Young Men, or family home evenings.

2. Many activities can be interchanged into other achievement areas. For example, the "Education and Scholarship" activity on a micro-environment hunt might easily be used to fulfill requirements in the "Outdoor Fun and Skills" category. You will discover a greater variety and flexibility as you familiarize yourself with all the activities in this book.

3. Consider the specific needs of your group when planning your activities. The number of children, their ages, the amount of time, and facilities are all important factors to success. These activities can easily be modified to fit your specific needs.

4. Parents and other adults in your ward are tremendous resources. Inquire about specific talents of these individuals and use them often! For example, if you know of someone who is interested in astronomy, enlist his or her help in the parent-and-child night activity. Always consider outside resources for help and expertise.

5. Family support will be a great help to your group. For this purpose, an achievement days calendar is offered in the back of the book. Regular use of this calendar will inform parents of the achievement goals their child is currently working on, as well as let them know of dates, times, and places. A sample calendar is also included to give you further details.

6. Most of the lessons have a "Family Ideas" section follow-up. These follow-up activities will help to increase parental involvement in this wonderful program. In addition they will enrich the children's experiences in each of the achievement areas. These ideas can also be listed on your family calendar.

7. To help with your recognition meetings, we have included several recognition certificates in the back of this book. You may desire to present the children with a certificate as they successfully complete the goals of each achievement section.

We know that as you apply these guidelines you will experience wonderful success.

Arts and Crafts

*To help me learn about the creative arts
and develop my artistic talents.*

If friends were like flowers I'd pick you!

Potpourri Shapes

Materials Needed

Cinnamon, flour, applesauce, cookie cutters, waxed paper, cutting boards, rolling pins, cookie sheets, pencil, ribbon or yarn.

Before You Meet

If this is an individual activity, have each child bring a mixing bowl and a 75-milliliter can of cinnamon.

Activity

- Combine 1/3 cup of flour and 1/3 cup of cinnamon (75-milliliter can) in a bowl.
- Add 2/3 of a cup of applesauce and continue to mix it all until completely blended. The dough will be very stiff.
- Place the dough on a cutting board and roll it out until it is 1/4″ thick.
- Cut out shapes with cookie cutters. This recipe will make about twelve shapes.
- Use the pencil to gently make a hole in the top of each shape.
- Line a cookie sheet with waxed paper.
- Place the shapes on the waxed paper and allow them to dry for two or three days.
- Thread a ribbon through the hole in each shape and tie it with an overhand or square knot.
- Give the shapes as gifts or hang them where they will fill the air with fragrance.

Making Sachets

Materials Needed

Lightweight cotton fabric in appropriate colors and prints for sachets, patterns (see "Before You Meet" below), chalk, several pairs of pinking shears, potpourri oil, cotton balls, wire twists (like those used to seal bread bags), 1/4"-wide fabric ribbon, small silk flowers, craft glue.

Before You Meet

Use lightweight poster board to make 10" x 10" square patterns.

Activity

- Put a few drops of potpourri oil on each cotton ball and then set them aside.
- Have the children trace the square pattern onto the fabric with a piece of chalk.
- Use pinking shears to cut out the square.
- Place four or five cotton balls onto the center of the square. Draw the edges of the square up around the cotton balls, forming a little bag. Use a wire twist to secure the fabric.
- Tie a ribbon under the twist. Fashion the ribbon into a bow, and trim the edges. Then remove the wire twist.
- Optional: Glue a silk flower onto the center of the bow.
- Sachets can be given for Christmas gifts, Mother's Day, or any other special occasion.

Making a Vase of Paper Flowers

Materials Needed

$5/8''$ buttons, light pink paper, pink paper, dark pink paper, red paper, green chenille stems (pipe cleaner), green tissue paper, scissors or pinking shears, all-purpose glue, glue stick.

Before You Meet

1. Cut the light pink paper into $2''$ squares, the pink paper into $2\,1/2''$ squares, the dark pink paper into $3''$ squares, the red paper into $3\,1/2''$ squares, and the green tissue into $4\,1/2''$ squares. Use other colors if you wish to add variety to the bouquet.
2. Make a flower to acquaint yourself with this craft.

Activity

- Give each child one square of each color of paper, one tissue square, a chenille stem, and one button.
- Insert the chenille stem through the bottom of the button until about two inches is on top. Bend it in half and carefully guide the stem down through another hole. Gently pull the button up to the chenille stem's bend, and then twist the stem until the button is secure.
- Have the children take the largest paper square and fold it into a triangle.

- Fold the paper in half two more times. Always keep the shape like a triangle.

- Holding the folded corner at the bottom, cut into an "ice-cream cone" shape. For a fancier edge use pinking shears. Cut a very small tip from the bottom of your "ice-cream cone."
- Unfold and gently flatten the paper. Your paper should look something like this:

- Repeat the process with each of the pink papers until all have been cut the same way.
- Fold the tissue the same way. Hold the folded corner at the bottom, and cut a deep scoop at the top.
- Glue the papers together, with the tissue on the bottom and the light pink paper on the top. Be careful to align the center holes and stagger the petal loops.
- Place a drop of all-purpose glue on the bottom of the button. Guide the chenille stem down through the center holes. Place the flower button-side down and gently press the petals onto the button.
- Let the flower stand upside down until dry.

Family Ideas

Have your child help make other flowers and take them to someone who is ill.

Table Place Mats

Materials Needed

11″ x 17″ colored paper, variety of colored markers, crayons, and pencils.

Before You Meet

1. Arrange to have the place mats laminated.
2. Note to leader: Consider making enough place mats to deliver to a special needs center, hospital, nursing home, or similar facility.

Activity

- Give each child an 11″ x 17″ piece of paper. Use markers, crayons, or colored pencils to decorate the paper. This can be done with a holiday, birthday, special person, or other theme of your choosing.
- Laminate the finished papers to make a personalized table place mat.

Wind Chime

Materials Needed

White spray paint. Provide for each child: one wide-mouth canning lid, four regular canning lids, three yards of brightly colored ¹/₈″ ribbon.

Before You Meet

1. Spray paint the canning lids.
2. Cut the ribbon into 12″ lengths.

Activity

- Tie four pieces of ribbon onto the wide-mouth canning lid. Space them equally and glue in place.

- Gather the four loose ends together and tie in an overhand knot.

- Tie a piece of ribbon onto each regular-sized canning lid.

- Attach the four regular rings evenly around the wide-mouth canning lid.

- Decorate, if you wish, by gluing small ribbons or silk flowers to the lids.

Family Ideas

As a family, make several wind chimes to give as gifts.

Cup-and-Saucer Flower Arrangement

Materials Needed

Matching cup and saucer for each child (thrift shops are an excellent resource for these), super-strength craft glue, florist foam, silk or dried flowers.

Before You Meet

1. Consider arranging for a specialist who is familiar with floral arranging to help you in this activity.
2. Use super-strength glue to affix cups in position onto saucers. Allow enough time for the glue to dry before the activity.

Activity

- Have the children fill their cups half full of florist foam.
- Push ends of silk or dried flowers into the florist foam to make a small bouquet. Start with larger flowers first, and add smaller ones such as baby's breath to fill in any empty spots.
- Glue a matching flower and baby's breath onto the saucer in front of the cup.

Family Ideas

Find a special place to display the cup-and-saucer bouquet.

Turkey Tray Decoration

Materials Needed

Two 3-ounce paper cups (either unwaxed or coated), one tongue depressor, four googly eyes, and two sheets of unlined paper for each child; crayons and sharpener, brown spray paint, craft glue, yellow and red acrylic paint, pencils, toothpicks, iron, scissors.

Before You Meet

1. Use a pencil or crayon sharpener to make crayon shavings. Use yellow, orange, and red crayons.
2. Spray paint the outside of the paper cups and both sides of the tongue depressor with brown paint.
3. Cut each tongue depressor into two 3″ lengths.
4. Use these tray decorations in association with a service activity, or have the children take them home as a decoration.

Activity

- Glue two googly eyes at the top of a tongue depressor half.
- Draw a diamond shape under the eyes and a teardrop under the diamond. Use toothpicks to paint the diamond yellow and the teardrop red. This completes the face and neck of the "turkey." Repeat the process with the second half of the tongue depressor.
- Turn the paper cups upside down, and glue a tongue depressor to the outside of each one, as shown. Allow the glue to dry thoroughly.
- Sprinkle crayon shavings between the two sheets of paper.
- To protect your iron, place the papers between several sheets of newsprint or two old towels and heat the paper until the crayon shavings melt. For the best results, use a blotting action to avoid smearing the colors. Afterward, immediately pull the two papers apart.
- Cut a 4″ diameter circle from one paper and a 2″ diameter circle from the other. Glue the smaller circle in the middle of the larger circle.

- Cut the glued circles in half.

- Cut the outside paper with slashes down to the beginning of the smaller circle to produce "tail feathers."

- Glue the tail feathers to the back of the cup.

9

Education and Scholarship

*To encourage me to succeed in school
and set goals for my education.*

Making Bookmarks

Materials Needed

Plastic needlepoint canvas, yarn, large-eyed needles, scissors. (For variety you can use different colors of canvas and yarn.)

Before You Meet

Cut the plastic canvas into 2″ x 6″ rectangles.

Activity

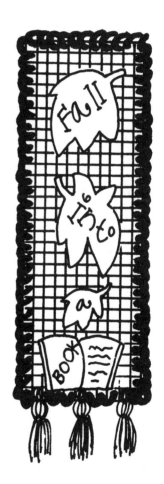

- Thread the needles with yarn. Help the children stitch around the edge of the plastic canvas. Begin by inserting the needle through the bottom corner square, then pull the yarn through, leaving a 1″ tail on the underneath side of the canvas. Wrap the yarn around the outside edge of the plastic canvas and back up through the next square. (Be sure to wrap the yarn around the 1″ tail to secure it in place.) Continue this pattern until all the edges of the canvas have been stitched around.
- To keep the yarn from unraveling, run the needle under three or four of the last stitches and pull the yarn through. Then trim off any excess yarn.
- Cut nine 7″ lengths of yarn for tassels. Thread one piece of yarn into a needle and go through the third square from the left above the border. Repeat with two more lengths into the same hole. Align all the yarn ends and tie them in a knot.
- Follow these directions to make two more tassels. Leave three empty squares between each tassel.
- Optional: Use stickers or additional stitching to decorate the bookmark.

Visiting an Animal Hospital

Materials Needed

Thank-you note, envelope, stamp, pen.

Before You Meet

1. Schedule a date and time for the group to tour an animal hospital. Explain that the objective of the field trip is to help the children understand the purposes of an animal hospital and learn how to better care for pets.
2. Provide for adequate transportation, if necessary. Fill out any travel permits required by your ward or stake.

Activity

- Take the children to the animal hospital.
- Be prepared to assist where needed.
- After returning from the animal hospital, write and send a thank-you note.

Family Ideas

Have your child share in family home evening what she has learned about pets. Talk about the love that Heavenly Father has for all his creations.

A Visit to the Museum

Before You Meet

1. Select a history or art museum to visit. Schedule a date and time for the group to tour the museum. Arrange for a guide, and inform your guide of your group's age and time considerations. Request pamphlets depicting some of the features of the museum.
2. Provide for adequate transportation, if necessary. Fill out any travel permits required by your ward or stake.

Activity

- Tour the museum.
- Invite the children to discuss their thoughts of the tour and share their favorite items.
- Distribute pamphlets depicting features of the museum for the children to take home.

Family Ideas

Provide a time to visit with your child about her tour of the museum. Review the pamphlet and let her share what she learned.

A Micro-Environment Hunt

Materials Needed

For each child: a magnifying glass and a 5' long string or yarn.

Before You Meet

Determine a place for this activity. Try to find a place that has a variety of small animals and plants.

Activity

- Have the children place their strings on the ground. Explain that this string will indicate their path through the micro-environment and that it need not be a straight line.
- Talk about pretending to be very small as they crawl along their path. Have them try to see the micro-world through the eyes of a very small creature. Tell the children that each of them will have a different experience and so it is important that they remember what they see.
- Give each child a magnifying glass, and have the hike begin.
- When the hike is over, gather the children and talk about what they saw and how they felt. If you desire, have the children draw a picture of their experience or write a page for their journal.

Family Ideas

Share your love of the natural world with your children. Take the family on a regular hike and discuss what you see.

A Visit to a New School

Before You Meet

1. Arrange for the children to visit the intermediate or junior high school they will be attending in the future. Request a short guided tour.
2. Provide for adequate transportation, if necessary. Fill out any travel permits required by your ward or stake.

Activity

- Tour the school.
- Invite the children to discuss their thoughts about going to a new school.

Family Ideas

Let your child share the experience of touring her future school. Discuss things she can do to be prepared for this change such as developing study skills, building friendships, and so on.

Making an Indoor Stargazer

Materials Needed

An empty round box (for example, a salt or oatmeal box) for every child, small nail, flashlight.

Before You Meet

1. Draw and label samples of several constellations (for example, the Big Dipper). To assist with this activity, ask a specialist to tell about the constellations or get information from a local library.
2. Make a sample stargazer to show the children what one will look like.

Activity

- Cut the top off of each round box.
- Draw a different constellation pattern on the bottom of each box.
- Use a nail to carefully make a hole for each star in the constellation.
- In a darkened room, shine a flashlight into the box and aim the box at the ceiling. The spots of light represent the stars of the constellation.
- Talk about where the constellations can be found in the sky and share any legends associated with that constellation.
- Send the stargazers home with the children.

Family Ideas

Have your child show her constellation to the family and talk about Heavenly Father's creations.

Family History

To help me learn about my family
and how we can be together forever.

A Personal Time Line

Materials Needed

Paper, pencils, rulers, stickers or markers, plastic sheet protectors.

Before You Meet

1. Have each child bring a list of important dates in her life.
2. Make your own time line so the children can see what one looks like.

Activity

- Explain what a time line is and what it shows.
- Give each child a piece of paper and have them draw a straight line lengthwise on the paper.
- Have each child write her birth date at the beginning of the line.
- Show the children how to enter their other important dates on a time line and have them proceed to do so.
- Decorate the time lines with stickers and markers.
- Place each child's time line into a plastic sheet protector, and challenge the children to put their time lines into a journal or personal history folder.

Family Ideas

Make a family time line. Go back as many generations as you want.

Ancestor Night

Materials Needed

Invitations and refreshments.

Before You Meet

1. Invite parents or other relatives to attend this activity with the children. Request that they be prepared to tell one or two stories about an ancestor.
2. Prepare refreshments.

Activity

- Take turns sharing ancestral stories.
- Talk about the stories and discuss what can be learned from them. Encourage the group to learn more about their personal family history.
- Serve refreshments.

Family Ideas

Compile a book of favorite stories about your ancestors. Set a goal to add one story a month.

Honoring Mother

Before You Meet

1. Ask the children to interview their mothers. Follow up with each child and be sure that each will have a presentation.
2. Contact each mother to prepare and bring a favorite food of her child. Use these favorites as refreshments.
3. If you desire, have the children make some kind of simple gift at a previous achievement day.

Activity

- After the opening prayer, have the children stand, one at a time, and tell about their mothers.
- When all of the children have honored their mothers, have a closing prayer and refreshments.

Family Ideas

Save the interview notes for your child's journal or keepsake book.

Learning About Other Cultures

Materials Needed

A world map, corkboard, pins, supplies required by specialist.

Before You Meet

1. Ask each child to bring the name of a country that some of her ancestors are from.
2. Arrange for a specialist to give a presentation to your group about the country that her ancestors are from. This can include traditions, food, work, recreation, and so on.
3. With the help of your specialist, prepare a food item from that country to serve as a refreshment.
4. Display the map on the corkboard.

Activity

- Help each child locate the country where her ancestors are from. Write her name on a small piece of paper and pin it to the map in the appropriate area.
- Introduce your guest speaker and explain that she will be sharing information about the country that some of her ancestors are from.
- Serve refreshments.
- Encourage the children to learn about their ancestral country.

Family Ideas

As a family learn about your ancestral country. Plan a family home evening discussing interesting traditions, playing games, and sharing a refreshment from that country.

A Family Photo Tree

Materials Needed

A copy of page 26 for each child, plastic sheet protectors, markers, glue, scissors.

Before You Meet

1. Talk with each child's parent and explain the purpose and needs of this activity. Each child will need to bring a picture of her parents and each brother and sister. Give the parent the option of sending photos or copies of photos. Explain that any pictures sent will not be reusable.
2. Make arrangements to pick up the pictures before the activity.
3. This activity can also be done with names and dates instead of photographs.
4. For the leader: Be sensitive to the needs of any child from a single-parent situation.

Activity

- Color the trees with the markers. Help the children understand the importance of taking their time and doing a good job.
- Cut the pictures to fit on the tree.
- Glue the parents' pictures on either side of the tree trunk.
- Give options on how to glue siblings' pictures on. For instance, place the pictures oldest to youngest, boys on left and girls on right, or in a mixed arrangement.
- After arranging the pictures, glue them in place.
- Place each photo tree inside a plastic sheet protector.

Family Ideas

Use the same idea to produce a larger family photo tree.

Journal Field Trip

Materials Needed

Supplies for games, refreshments, "A Special Day" form for each child (see page 28), a writing surface (such as a tabletop, lapboard, or book), and pencils.

Before You Meet

1. Schedule a time and date to take your group to a local park or recreational area.
2. Plan two or three games, such as jump rope, relays, or dodge ball.
3. Prepare simple refreshments.
4. Provide for adequate transportation, if necessary. Fill out any travel permits required by your ward or stake.

Activity

- Discuss safety rules and guidelines with your group at the park.
- Play the games you have selected.
- Enjoy a short free-play time.
- Serve refreshments.
- Pass out copies of "A Special Day" and pencils. Help each child fill out her journal sheet.
- Discuss the importance of keeping journals to help us remember special times.

Family Ideas

Set aside some time each week to record family events in a family journal.

A Special Day

Date:

Today I went to:

The weather was:

Some things I did:

My favorite thing was:

My least favorite thing was:

People who were with me:

I would/would not want to do this again because:

Letter to a Relative

Materials Needed

Stationery, envelopes, pencils, stamps.

Before You Meet

Ask each child to bring the name and address of a relative whom she would like to write a letter to (preferably a relative she is not able to see regularly).

Activity

- Discuss the importance of families. Explain that part of family history is getting to know and strengthening our extended family members now.
- Help the children write letters to the persons they have chosen.
- Address, stamp, and mail the letters.

Family Ideas

Encourage your child to continue to correspond with her extended family.

Family Skills

*To give me opportunities to help my
family now and in the future.*

Housekeeping Skills

Materials Needed

Vacuum, broom, dustpan, furniture polish, glass cleaner, cleaning cloths.

Before You Meet

Determine a home to meet in to teach basic housekeeping skills.

Activity

- Teach the group how to vacuum a room. Talk to them about covering all the floor surface, not vacuuming up small objects, plugging and unplugging carefully, not running over the cord, and winding the cord up. Let them take turns trying vacuuming.
- Teach the children how to sweep a room. Talk about moving items so you can sweep underneath them, sweeping the entire floor surface, and picking up debris with a dustpan. Let each child practice.
- Teach the group how to dust. Give instructions on carefully taking objects off the shelves, wiping the entire surface area, using furniture polish, and replacing objects on the shelves. Let the children take turns trying this.
- Instruct the group on cleaning mirrors and windows. Discuss the use of a glass cleaner and the importance of wiping the entire surface. Let each child practice.

Family Ideas

Make a chore chart and let your child demonstrate the housekeeping skills she has developed.

Developing Communication and Cooperation Skills

Materials Needed

Any materials necessary for the selected activities.

Before You Meet

Select three or more of the games described below. Be sensitive to the needs and abilities of the children.

Activity

- Briefly discuss the concepts of communication and cooperation. Explain how these two skills influence many areas of our life and why it is important to develop them.
- Play each selected game.

Verbal Communication 1: Divide the children into pairs, and have them sit back to back. Give Person One a picture with two or three interconnecting shapes and Person Two a pencil and paper. Using verbal description only, Person One must help his partner draw a duplicate of the picture. After a specified length of time, switch roles.

Verbal Communication 2: Divide the children into pairs, and blindfold one person in each pair. The blindfolded child must follow her partner's verbal instruction to accomplish some simple task, such as stacking several blocks, putting lids on several different-sized jars, walking through a maze, and so forth.

Back-to-Back Race: Mark a course of about thirty yards. Divide everyone into groups of three, and have each group link their elbows together to form a small circle, with their backs to the inside of the circle. The children in each group must work together to get to the finish line first.

Feather Race: Mark a course of about thirty feet. Divide the children into pairs, and give each pair one feather. Using only their breath, each pair must blow their feather into the air and keep it there until they have moved it over the finish line.

Mirror Race: Use a course of about thirty yards. Divide your group into pairs, and give each pair a small, hand-held mirror. Person One, who is facing away from the course, will place her hands on her partner's shoulders. Her partner, Person Two, is facing the course and holding the mirror. The mirror should be held so that Person One can see the course behind her. Each pair of children can use only the mirror to guide them to the finish line. (Allowing the partners to talk to each other is optional.) Repeat so that each person has the chance to hold the mirror.

Three-legged Walk: Mark a course of about thirty yards. Pair off the children. Tie one person's right leg to her partner's left leg. Have each team try to walk as rapidly as possible to the finish line.

Easy Snacks

Materials Needed

Ingredients required in recipes, poster board, markers, recipe cards, pencils, small paper plates, cups, napkins.

Before You Meet

1. Make grape juice ice cubes as specified in the Grape Fizz recipe.

    Grape Fizz
    Mix one can of frozen grape juice concentrate according to the directions on the can. Pour the juice into ice cube trays and freeze. Remove the frozen juice cubes from the trays. Put two cubes in each glass, and pour lemon-lime soda pop over cubes. Serve immediately.

    Fruit and Dip
    Mix one package of instant lemon pudding according to the directions on the box. Chill. Slice a variety of fruits, such as bananas, apples, pineapple, grapes, or oranges. Arrange the fruit on a tray. Use toothpicks to dip the fruit slices into the lemon pudding dip before eating.

    Crackers and Cheese
    Mix one package of powdered dip mix (any flavor) into a 24-ounce container of cottage cheese. Put one teaspoon of cottage cheese mixture on a snack cracker. Arrange crackers topped with seasoned cottage cheese on a tray.

2. Using the markers, write the recipes for the three snacks on the poster board.

Activity

- Display the prepared poster board. Pass out the recipe cards and pencils. Help the children write the recipes on cards.
- Teach the children how to make the Fruit and Dip snack. Instruct them on proper ways to slice fruit.
- Teach the group how to prepare the Crackers and Cheese snack. Let everyone help top the crackers.
- Teach the group how to make the Grape Fizz drink using the prepared grape juice cubes.
- Enjoy the snacks together as a group.
- Send each child's recipe cards home with her.

Family Ideas

Let your child share what she learned by preparing refreshments for an upcoming family home evening.

A Children's Puzzle and Game

Materials Needed

Coloring book with simple pictures, markers, heavy paper, ten plain index cards for each child, rubber cement or other paper glue, clear contact paper, pencils, scissors, re-sealable plastic bags.

Before You Meet

1. Make an example of each project to show the children.
2. Cut the contact paper into paper-sized squares.
3. To the leader: You can simplify the puzzle section of this activity by selecting two or three simple pictures and copying them onto heavy paper. If you choose to do this, delete the second step.

Activity

Making a Puzzle
- Allow each child to select a picture from the coloring books and color it with markers.
- Glue each colored picture to a piece of heavy paper. Rubber cement is the best for this project and dries quickly but may not be appropriate for your group.
- While the glue is drying, you can either talk about marking and cutting the pictures into puzzle shapes or you can begin to make the game.
- Carefully cover the front of each picture with the clear contact paper.
- Draw a cutting pattern on the back of each picture. Then cover the back of the picture with contact paper.
- Follow the previously drawn lines and cut each puzzle piece apart. Place the puzzle pieces in a plastic bag.

Making a Matching Game
- Draw a different shape on each of five index cards. Repeat the shapes on the other five cards. When finished, each child should have five different pairs of shapes.
- Color each pair a different color. (If the markers bleed through the cards, use crayons or colored pencils instead.)
- Place the finished matching game into another plastic bag.
- If time permits, place all the children's matching game sets face down on a large flat surface and play a group game.

Family Ideas

Add the puzzle and game to a baby-sitting kit.

Making Craft Dough

Materials Needed

Stove, ingredients for dough, large pot, measuring cups, measuring spoons, stirring spoon, plastic bags, poster board, marker, recipe cards, pencils.

Before You Meet

Copy the following recipe onto a poster board:
- 1 cup flour
- 2 teaspoons cream of tartar
- $^1/_2$ teaspoon salt
- 1 cup of water
- 1 tablespoon vegetable oil
- 15 drops of your favorite food coloring

Cook all ingredients in a pot over medium heat, stirring hard for about 4 minutes or until mixture forms a ball. Remove the ball of dough from the pot and let it cool for five minutes. Knead the dough for 30 seconds or until it is smooth and its color is blended. Cool completely. Store in an airtight container in the refrigerator.

Activity

- Follow the recipe to make a batch of dough for each child.
- Cool the dough as directed.
- Let the children knead the dough thoroughly. Let dough cool completely.
- Pass out recipe cards and pencils. Display the prepared poster board. Help the children copy the recipe.
- When the dough is cool, let the children play with it for a few minutes. Remind them to store it tightly sealed in the refrigerator. Point out that they can share it with the family or use it when baby-sitting.
- Have each child take home a bag of craft dough and a recipe card.

Family Ideas

Make enough dough for the entire family. Enjoy this activity together.

Making a Recipe File

Materials Needed

Index cards, hole punch, 2 hinged rings for each child, scissors, glue, ingredients for activity recipe.

Before You Meet

1. Contact a parent of each child and ask for a simple recipe that is used by the family. Suggest a non-dessert recipe. Make arrangements to pick these up a week before the activity.
2. Make a copy of each recipe for every child.
3. Choose a simple casserole, salad, or biscuit recipe for the activity.

Activity

- Discuss with the children the importance of recipes.
- Prepare the activity recipe. Read each step of the recipe aloud, and give every child the opportunity to help in some way.
- As the casserole (or whatever) cooks, have the children cut the family recipes out and glue them to the index cards.
- Punch two holes in the top of each recipe card, and assemble the file by inserting the hinged rings through the holes.

Family Ideas

Give your child the opportunity to prepare one of the recipes from her file. Help her as necessary.

Health and Personal Grooming

*To help me keep the Word of Wisdom
and be an example of Latter-day Saint
cleanliness, grooming, and modesty.*

Making a Good-Food Collage

Materials Needed

Provide for each child: magazines, scissors, $1/2$ poster board, glue stick.

Before You Meet

You may wish to use this activity as a follow-up for "Learning About the Food Pyramid," page 45.

Activity

- Briefly review with the children any ideas about eating good food.
- Explain that a collage covers the entire area of a poster board with many kinds of pictures. Tell the children that this will be a collage about food that makes our bodies healthy.
- Allow time for each child to complete a collage.
- Display their collages at a recognition night.

Visiting an Eye Doctor

Materials Needed

A thank-you card, envelope, pen, stamp.

Before You Meet

1. Schedule a convenient time for your group to tour the office of an optometrist or ophthalmologist. Request a presentation on good eye care and prevention of eye injuries. Ask for a pamphlet that each child can take home.
2. Provide for adequate transportation, if necessary. Fill out any travel permits required by your ward or stake.

Activity

- Tour the optometrist or ophthalmologist office.
- Have the presentation on good eye care and prevention of eye injuries.
- Let your group sign and mail a thank-you card following this activity.

Family Ideas

Review the eye care pamphlet as a family.

Healthy-Body Posters

Materials Needed

A poster board for each child, pencils, rulers, markers.

Before You Meet

Contact each child and ask her to bring an inexpensive but healthy treat for the activity. Ask her to bring enough to share with all in the group.

Activity

- Talk about how to keep a body healthy. Some ideas may include eating well, exercising, getting enough sleep, and so forth.
- Give each child a poster board and invite them to make posters that encourage other people to take care of their bodies.
- Display the posters at the next recognition night.

Family Ideas

Help your family develop habits to stay healthy.

Skin Care

Materials Needed

Those required by your specialist, thank-you card, envelope, stamp, pen.

Before You Meet

Make arrangements for a nurse or other health-care professional to give a presentation to your group about protective skin care. This should include avoiding overexposure to sun, heat, and cold; using protective items such as sunscreen, hats, and gloves; maintaining cleanliness; and treating surface irritations like scrapes, dryness, and insect bites.

Activity

- Welcome and introduce your guest.
- Receive her presentation on skin care.
- Sign and mail the thank-you card to your guest speaker.

Family Ideas

Let your child share what she has learned about good skin care with your family.

Learning About the Food Pyramid

Materials Needed

Any materials needed by the specialist.

Before You Meet

1. Invite a specialist to teach the children about the food pyramid. Define goals and time limits for your specialist. Follow up to help as necessary.
2. Contact each child and have her bring a healthy snack to share with all in the group.

Activity

- Gather the children and introduce your guest.
- Listen to your specialist's presentation about the food pyramid.
- Give the children the opportunity to ask questions and make comments.
- Pass the snacks around.

Family Ideas

Show how you can use the food pyramid to plan meals for the family.

Word of Wisdom Skits

Materials Needed

Simple props as needed in skits, paper, pencils.

Before You Meet

1. This activity may be divided into several meetings: planning and writing skits, practice, and performance. The objective of the skits is to give the children an opportunity to role-play situations that involve the Word of Wisdom.
2. Arrange for an assistant if you need additional help.
3. Plan a date, time, and location for the performance. You may want to consider a recognition night. This would be an excellent opportunity to show parents what the children have been learning.

Activity

- Prepare simple skits. Include in the skits the various ways that we are enticed to use tobacco, alcohol, or drugs, such as through television, music, friends, books, magazines, and so on. Help the children come up with creative ways to resist these temptations and say no. Remember that the planning and practice will be as educational as the performance.
- Assign all the parts, and include all the children.
- Plan and prepare simple props.
- Practice.
- Give the performance.

Family Ideas

Encourage your child to fulfill her assignment for the skits. Be sure to go to the performance.

Hospitality

To help me learn how I can have good relationships with others and how I can help others be comfortable in groups.

Recognition Night

Materials Needed

Invitations, ingredients for refreshments, award certificates.

Before You Meet

1. Prepare invitations and send them home with the children.
2. Prepare refreshments with the children (see "Easy Snacks" on page 35 for a preceding activity).
3. Prepare award certificates (see pages 119–123 for award certificate forms).
4. Meet with the children to plan the agenda for the meeting. Include the following:

   Opening Song
   Prayer (child)
   Welcome (child)
   Musical presentation (group)
   Two talks on "My Favorite Achievement Day Activity" (children)
   Presentation of achievement day awards (leader)
   Closing song
   Prayer (child)
   Refreshments

5. Delegate some children to arrive early to help set up for the meeting, and assign others to help clean up.

Activity

- Set up for the meeting.
- Have the recognition meeting as outlined.
- Clean up.

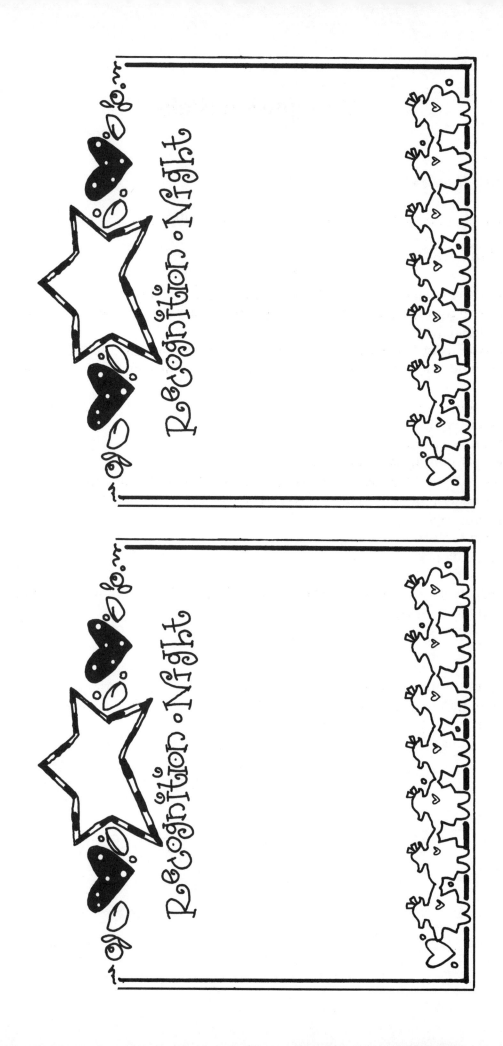

Recognition·Night

Recognition·Night

Making Gift Bags

Materials Needed

Brightly colored calendar pictures or similar pictures, small paper bags, pencils, scissors, glue stick, hole reinforcers, hole punch, yarn, wrapping tissue.

Before You Meet

Cut yarn into 14″ lengths.

Activity

- Decide on the kind of shape you want to put on your bag. Draw two large and six small patterns on a calendar picture of your choice.
- Cut out the designs.
- Glue one large and three small designs to each side of the paper bag.
- Punch two holes at the top on each side of the paper bag.
- Place hole reinforcers around each punched hole.
- Thread one length of yarn through a hole, back to front, and back through the other hole on the same side of the bag. Tie the two ends together in a square or overhand knot.
- Repeat with the other length of yarn on the opposite side.
- Show the children how to place the tissue in their gift bags.
- You may want to use this activity in connection with "Wrapping Presents" on page 55.

Family Ideas

Encourage your child to make and use these bags as an economical way of wrapping gifts.

Writing Letters to Pen Pals

Materials Needed

Stationery, envelopes, pencils, stamps.

Before You Meet

1. With the help of a Primary president or achievement days leader from another area, obtain the names and addresses of children whom your group can be pen pals with. You will need a pen pal for each member of your group.
2. Prepare to teach the children how to write a letter and address an envelope.

Activity

- Teach the group how to write a letter. Include date, greeting, introduction, items of interest, and closing.
- Give instructions on the correct way to address the envelope and place the stamp.
- Give each child the name and address of her pen pal. Help the children write their letters and address the envelopes.
- Mail the letters.

Family Ideas

Encourage your child to continue corresponding with her pen pal.

A Manners Fair

Materials Needed

Check selected exhibits for materials needed.

Before You Meet

1. Involve other adults in setting up for and carrying out this activity.
2. Make signs for each exhibit.
3. If you desire, invite another achievement day group or have it as a family activity.

Activity

- Discuss with the children the importance of manners in everyday living. Help them understand that good manners affect the way we treat each other.
- Direct the children to the exhibits. The following exhibits are suggestions only:

  Introductions: Demonstrate how to introduce people to each other. Allow every child the opportunity to make an introduction.
  Telephone Skills: See page 73.
  Thank-you Notes: Briefly discuss the concept of gratitude. Give each child a plain, undecorated note card and have her decorate it. Challenge her to send it to someone she appreciates.
  Table Manners: Have a table set for the children. Serve some simple food items. Practice asking for and passing food items, cutting with a fork and a knife (try celery), using napkins, buttering bread, and so forth.
  Courtesy for Older People: Practice ways to show courtesy for older people—holding doors open for them, speaking to them with respect, helping them up stairs. Help the children understand that not all older people appreciate or need this kind of help, so the children must be sensitive to needs.
  Concert and Movie Manners: Talk about the importance of listening at a concert and explain about intermissions, applause, and so forth.

A Seniors Social

Materials Needed

Invitations, table decorations, refreshments.

Before You Meet

1. Meet with your group to plan and organize a seniors social. Plan table decorations, refreshments, and entertainment. Make the necessary assignments. Discuss what it means to be a good host or hostess. Remind them that the objective is to make sure their guests feel welcome and enjoy themselves.
2. Plan the date, time, place, and guest list. As a group make and deliver invitations.

Activity

- Set up and prepare before the guests arrive.
- Welcome and seat the guests.
- Serve refreshments.
- Mingle and visit.
- Provide entertainment.
- Thank the guests for coming.
- Clean up.

Family Ideas

Discuss ways you can make people feel welcome and comfortable in your home. Invite someone special to have dinner with your family and practice these hospitality skills.

Wrapping Presents

Materials Needed

Inexpensive wrapping paper, empty boxes, tape, ribbon.

Before You Meet

1. If you desire, involve another adult to help you teach the children this skill.
2. Use this activity as a supplement to "Making Gift Bags" (see page 51).

Activity

- Give each child an empty box.
- Teach the children how to determine how much wrapping paper to use. Allow the children, with supervision, to measure and cut the wrapping paper they need.
- Take the children step-by-step through the basic wrapping process.
- Show them one or two ways to decorate with ribbon, and have them decorate their own packages with the ribbons.
- These wrapped presents could be used as decorations for a daddy-daughter or a miss-and-mom party.

Family Ideas

Have your child help wrap family gifts.

Outdoor Fun
and Skills

*To learn skills that will help me enjoy
the creations of our Father in Heaven.*

Parent-and-Child Night Activity

Materials Needed

A large, open area or park away from city lights.

Before You Meet

1. Reserve or otherwise arrange to use the park.
2. Make invitations and have the children deliver to their parents.
3. Invite a specialist to talk about stars or constellations. Ask him or her to be prepared to identify and show locations for two or three. Give specific information about time limits and group size.
4. Have the children bring a blanket large enough for parents and child.
5. If you desire, you may use this activity as a recognition night.

Activity

- Have any recognition night activities first.
- Turn the time over to your guest specialist.
- Allow time for questions or comments.
- Spend time finding constellations in the night sky.

Family Ideas

Have a family stargazing activity or visit a planetarium.

"Follow the Leader" Walk

Materials Needed

A whistle, healthy snacks and drinks (such as fresh fruit and juice), cups, napkins.

Before You Meet

1. Select a location for your walk that is free from traffic and other hazards. The walk should be one mile from start to finish. Choose a spot near the end of your course to serve refreshments.
2. Contact the children before the activity to remind them to wear comfortable shoes and clothing for the walk.
3. Make transportation arrangements to return the children home after the walk.

Activity

- Prepare your group for the one-mile "Follow the Leader" walk. The children should be in a single-file line. The first person in line is the leader. As the children walk, the leader will add variations for the group to do—singing, marching, clapping, and so on. Explain to the children that you will follow from behind with a whistle. When you blow the whistle, the leader goes to the end of the line, and the next person becomes the new leader. This pattern will continue for the entire walk.
- Follow the designated route for your one-mile walk. Change leaders often for variety.
- Serve refreshments when you reach your destination. While the children are having the snack, discuss with them the importance of exercise. Point out that exercising with friends is often more enjoyable than exercising alone.

Family Ideas

Plan a "Follow the Leader" one-mile walk as an activity for family home evening. Let your child take charge and explain how it is done.

Learning About Dutch-Oven Cooking

Materials Needed

Plates, forks, Dutch ovens, and any other items necessary for this activity (depending on the menu, for example).

Before You Meet

1. Decide on one or two simple recipes that can be prepared during this demonstration.
2. If you desire, invite a specialist to be in charge of this activity. Be sure to give specific information, such as purpose, time limits, expected attendance, and so forth.

Activity

- Demonstrate how to put the recipe ingredients into the Dutch oven. Have the children help as much as possible.
- While the food is cooking, talk about the correct use of Dutch ovens. Be sure to include proper cleanup.
- When the food is finished cooking, sample each recipe.
- Demonstrate cleanup. If possible, have the children help with any cleanup necessary.
- Encourage the children to share with their families what they learned.

Outdoor Bubbles

Materials Needed

Wire coat hangers, pliers, old cotton fabric torn into one-inch strips, dishwashing liquid (quality brand), glycerin (available at drugstores), water, a large pan or tub.

Before You Meet

1. Mix up bubble solution using the following recipe: 5 cups of water, $1/2$ cup of dishwashing liquid, $1/8$ cup of pure glycerin. Change proportionately to fit your needs. Pour it into a tub or pan that is large enough to immerse the coat hanger hoops.
2. Use pliers to shape the coat hangers into bubble hoops. Squeeze together the hooked end of the hanger so that it's flat and forms a handle. Shape the hooped section of the hanger into a circle. Bend the handle up so it will be easier to dip the hoop into the bubble solution. Make sure the hoop is as flat as possible.

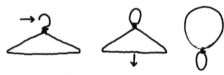

3. Note: this activity requires a still day because too much wind can pop bubbles.

Activity

- Pass out coat hanger hoops and strips of cloth to each child. Wrap the strips of cloth around the wire hoop, overlapping the edges. Tie off the ends of the cloth at the handle. The cloth helps to absorb the bubble solution to make big bubbles. Trim off any strings or ends that could pop the bubbles.
- Demonstrate to the children how to make the big bubbles. Lay the hoop flat in the solution and let it soak for a few seconds. Don't slosh hoops around, as it will create foam. Turn the hoop on its side (vertical) while it is still in the solution. Lift it up and slowly wave your hoop through the air to make a tube, then twist your wrist to twist the end of the bubble off your hoop. If your movements are too quick it will break the bubble film.
- Take turns making bubbles. Caution the children to keep their hands out of the solution as the soap can be irritating to their skin. Occasionally skim off any foam that develops on the bubble solution. Be sure to thoroughly wash everyone's hands following the activity to remove any bubble solution.

Family Ideas

Plan a special family night to make big bubbles.

A Five-Senses Hunt

Materials Needed

Paper, pencils.

Before You Meet

1. Contact each child and ask her to bring a towel.
2. Make any arrangements necessary to use a park or outdoor area for this activity.

Activity

- Give each child a pencil and a piece of paper.
- Have the children write the five senses (touch, hear, taste, see, smell) across the top of the paper.
- Designate a particular area for this activity. Although the children should be separated, it is still necessary for the leader(s) to be able to see the children at all times. Explain to the children that they may list only the things they can see, hear, feel, and so on from their personal place. Remind them that this is to be a quiet time so they can use all of their senses. Set a time limit.
- Have every child choose a space within the activity area and use her towel to sit on.
- Gather the children at the end of the time limit and have them share some of the things they discovered.

Chalk Murals

Materials Needed

Sidewalk chalk.

Before You Meet

Select a location for drawing the sidewalk murals.

Activity

- Discuss with the group what a mural is. Explain that it is a large picture that is painted or drawn on a flat surface such as a wall or sidewalk. Encourage the children to think about what kind of picture they would like to draw before they begin.
- Designate a spot for each child to draw a mural. Put the sidewalk chalk in a handy location for all of the children to use. As they are drawing, remind them to use lots of color and detail for an exciting picture.
- Have the children initial their pictures.
- As a group, view each child's mural. Have them describe it to you.

Family Ideas

Go and see the murals as a family. Let your child tell you about each one.

Flying Kites

Materials Needed

A kite and string for each child.

Before You Meet

1. Select a large open area that is appropriate for flying kites. It should be free of trees, power lines, and other hazards.
2. Arrange for other adults to help you with this activity.

Activity

- Teach the group about the appropriate areas for kite flying. Discuss the hazards of power lines, trees, and so on.
- Explain how to launch a kite into the air, control it, and bring it down.
- Help the children fly their kites.

Family Ideas

Allow your child to share what she has learned about flying kites. Plan a family outing to fly kites.

Personal Preparedness

*To develop personal habits and skills
that will help me provide for myself.*

Reusable Goal Chart

Materials Needed

Copies of goal chart (see page 70), markers, stickers and other craft items as desired, a transparency marker for each child.

Before You Meet

1. Be prepared to discuss goal setting with your group.
2. Look at the sample goal sheet (see page 70) to help you in teaching your group how to decorate their own personal goal charts.
3. Make arrangements for the goal charts to be laminated.

Activity

- Discuss the importance of goals. Give examples of specific goals, such as practicing the piano 20 minutes each day for a month, reading for 15 minutes each night for a month, doing a good deed each day, and so on. Teach the children about setting goals and keeping track of their progress.
- Pass out copies of the goal sheets. Children should write their first name across the top border. Help the children decorate the borders of the goal sheets. Consider using stickers, coloring with markers, gluing on confetti or other cutouts, and so on.
- Laminate the goal charts.
- Demonstrate to the children how to use their goal charts. First, decide what goal they are going to work on. Use a transparency marker to fill in the goal and the date in the appropriate blanks. Second, use their transparency marker to check off each day that they successfully kept their goal. When the chart is completed, use a damp cloth to wipe off. Select a new goal and reuse the chart.

Family Ideas

Help your child find a good place to display her chart. Encourage her to use it for personal goals.

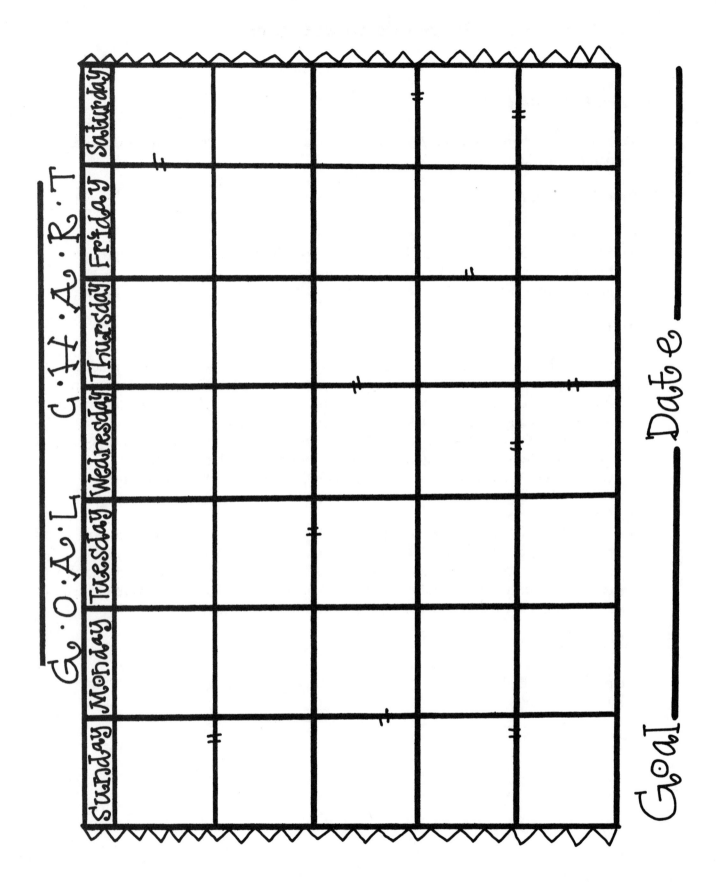

G·O·A·L C·H·A·R·T

Sunday	Monday	Tuesday	Wednesday	Thursday	Friday	Saturday

Goal _____

Date _____

Miriam's

G·O·A·L G·H·A·R·T

Sunday	Monday	Tuesday	Wednesday	Thursday	Friday	Saturday
1	2	3	4	5	6	7
8	9	10	11	12	13	14
15	16	17	18	19	20	21
22	23	24	25	26	27	28
29	30	31				

keep going!

Goal Practice Piano Date MARCH

Planting a Tomato Bowl

Materials Needed

Gravel, potting soil, cherry tomato seedlings, marigold seedlings.

Before You Meet

Ask each child to bring a twelve-inch flowerpot.

Activity

- Have each child place about one inch of gravel at the bottom of her pot. Cover the gravel with potting soil until the pot is about half full.
- Place the tomato seedling in the center of the pot and arrange two or three marigold plants around the outer edge.
- Fill in all the remaining areas with potting soil. Gently but firmly pack the soil in place.
- Water thoroughly.
- Talk to the children about caring for their tomato bowl. If one of the children does not like tomatoes, have her provide a service by growing them and then sharing with a neighbor.

Family Ideas

Help remind your child to care for her tomato bowl. You may wish to use this experience to teach your child about developing a testimony (see Alma 32:28–29).

Telephone Skills

Materials Needed

Two or more disconnected phones, phone books, notepads, pencils.

Before You Meet

Contact your local phone company to get information about teaching children to properly use the phone.

Activity

- Pass out a phone book to each child. Familiarize them with its contents, such as emergency and special service numbers, white pages, yellow pages, and so on.
- Teach the children how to look up residential phone numbers. Have them find their own number and that of another family member or friend.
- Teach the group how to use the yellow pages. Practice looking up businesses of your choice.
- Give the children instructions on answering the phone and taking messages. Practice this on disconnected phones. Include the following: what information to give or not give to the caller, being polite, writing down the information, and giving the message to the appropriate person promptly.

Family Ideas

Let your child practice her telephone answering skills. Keep a notepad and pencil close to the phone.

Visiting a Preschool

Materials Needed

Thank-you card, envelope, and stamp.

Before You Meet

1. Make arrangements to visit a local preschool or day-care center. Ask for someone who will talk about child care as a vocation. Give specific information about time limits and group size.
2. Provide for adequate transportation, if necessary. Fill out any travel permits required by your ward or stake.

Activity

*   Tour the preschool facilities.
*   Listen to the presentation, and let the children ask questions and make comments.
*   Let your group sign and mail a thank-you card following the activity.

Family Ideas

As a family, discuss ways to develop the patience and love important in a child-care situation. Help your children understand that these same characteristics are important in developing an eternal family.

Planting Flowers

Materials Needed

Flower seedlings, hand spades, watering can.

Before You Meet

1. Select a location for this service, such as a church, library, or ward member's home.
2. Be prepared to teach the children how to plant flower seedlings. Contact a local nursery if needed for advice.
3. Request that each child bring a six-pack of flower seedlings. You may want to recommend several hardy varieties in your area.

Activity

- Prepare the ground for planting. Remove any weeds and debris, and break up the soil.
- Dig holes as specified for the seedlings.
- Remove the flowers from their containers and set them in the holes.
- Add some water to the holes and then fill in with dirt around the plants. Press the dirt firmly into place.
- Consider returning occasionally to care for the plants.

Family Ideas

Select a small area for your child to grow her own flowers.

Visiting a Small Business

Materials Needed

Thank-you card, envelope, and stamp.

Before You Meet

1. Make any arrangements necessary to visit a local small business. Ask the owner, or another representative, to discuss the importance of planning and education. You may also ask the owner to talk about the characteristics of a good employee. Be sure to let him know of specific time restraints.
2. Provide for adequate transportation, if necessary. Fill out any travel permits required by your ward or stake.

Activity

- If appropriate, tour the facilities and see how the product is made or how the type of services is made available to customers.
- Listen to the presentation. Allow time for questions from the children.
- Let your group sign and mail a thank-you card following the activity.

Family Ideas

Use information about education to encourage a positive effort in school.

Safety and Emergency Preparedness

To learn how to be safe and what to do in emergencies.

A Visit to a Police Station

Materials Needed

Thank-you card, envelope, stamp, pen.

Before You Meet

1. Schedule a date and time for the group to tour a local police station. Ask if the children can receive a child fingerprint record and make the necessary arrangements to do so.
2. Encourage the children to prepare questions for the tour.
3. Provide for adequate transportation, if necessary. Fill out any travel permits required by your ward or stake.

Activity

- Tour the police station.
- Help the children obtain child fingerprint records.
- Let your group sign and mail the thank-you card after the activity.

Family Ideas

Place your child's fingerprint record with other important family papers.

Visiting the Electric Company

Materials Needed

Thank-you card, envelope, stamp, pen.

Before You Meet

1. Contact the local power company and arrange a brief tour for your group. Request a discussion on electrical safety rules. Ask for pamphlets that the children can take home.
2. Provide for adequate transportation, if necessary. Fill out any travel permits required by your ward or stake.

Activity

- Tour the electrical company.
- Listen to the presentation of electrical safety rules.
- Have the children take the pamphlets home.
- Help the children sign and mail the thank-you card.

Family Ideas

Read and discuss the pamphlet as a family. Evaluate your safety procedures.

Learning About Emergency Phone Numbers

Materials Needed

Copies of "Emergency Phone Numbers" (see page 82) for each child, small stickers, markers, bright yellow or bright red paper.

Before You Meet

1. Cut the bright paper in half.
2. Create emergency and nonemergency ideas for the children to discuss.

Activity

- Talk about making an emergency phone call. Include specifics about when it is necessary and how to make that decision. Explain the importance of having the correct address to give the emergency dispatcher.
- Use specific situations to make points. For instance, "Your little brother is crying and you can't make him stop," or "Your friend fell out of a tree and has broken her arm."
- Follow each situation with a brief discussion. Help the children understand how important it is to not call 911 unless it is a real emergency.
- Give each child an "Emergency Phone Numbers" paper, and, using your master copy, have them fill in the blanks. Tell them that the "Other Numbers" should be filled in after they talk with their parents. These numbers might include those of grandparents, neighbors, home teachers, and others. Explain that every child must put her address in large, neat letters.

Family Ideas

Help your child complete her emergency phone list, and place it where it can be easily seen.

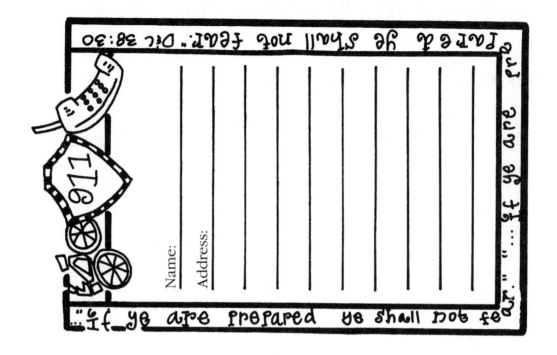

911

"...If ye are prepared ye shall not fear." D&C 38:30

Name:
Address:

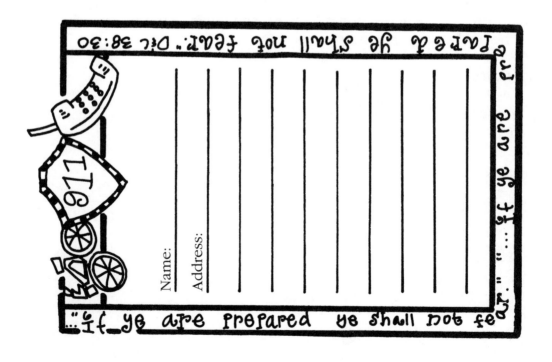

911

"...If ye are prepared ye shall not fear." D&C 38:30

Name:
Address:

Kitchen Safety

Materials Needed

Pot, casserole pan, spoon, vegetable peeler, hot pads, carrots, celery.

Before You Meet

1. Make arrangements to use a kitchen.
2. Be prepared to give a presentation on kitchen safety. Contact your county extension office for detailed information and pamphlets.

Activity

- With the oven turned *off,* demonstrate how to put a casserole dish into the oven and how to remove it. Discuss using hot pads, sliding oven racks out, and having a prepared place to set the hot casserole dish.
- With the stove burners turned *off,* demonstrate how to heat items on the stove. Discuss keeping handles turned towards stove center, holding handles while stirring, not leaving spoons in pans, and keeping clothing away from burners.
- Discuss peeling and slicing techniques. Demonstrate peeling and slicing carrots and celery. Remind them to keep their fingers out of the way and to take their time.
- Role-play kitchen safety habits. Have each child take a turn demonstrating what she has learned. Praise the appropriate actions, and make corrections when needed.
- Review safety techniques as you share carrot and celery sticks. Brainstorm other kitchen safety ideas.
- Give each child a kitchen safety pamphlet to take home.

Family Ideas

Review the kitchen safety pamphlet with your child. Help her to prepare a meal, focusing on safety in the kitchen.

Practicing Self-Protection

Before You Meet

1. Prayerfully decide on the best situations for your group to role-play. Be sensitive to the needs of each child. Use situations listed in this activity or others of your own choosing.
2. Make a copy of the situations listed below and give it to each child's parent. Encourage the discussion of safety in family home evening.

Activity

- Go through every situation and talk about the correct action or response to each one. You can do this by giving multiple-choice answers, by having them guess, or by telling them.
- Role-play each chosen situation.
  1. Someone comes to your house and tells you that he is a plumber and needs to fix your plumbing. What should you do? (If you are alone, never open the door to a stranger. Ask to see identification.)
  2. A phone call is for a parent, but you are home alone. What should you say? (Indicate that the parent is busy and will return the call. Do NOT tell the caller that you are alone.)
  3. You have lost track of your parents in a busy mall and do not know where to find them. What should you do? (Look for a mall security officer, an information booth, or a mother with young children.)
  4. You are at a friend's house, and she invites you to go with her parent to a store. How should you handle this? (Call and get permission from your parent. If you cannot reach a guardian, return home.)
  5. You answer the phone, and someone on the other end begins swearing or using obscene language. What should you say? (Don't say anything. Hang up immediately. If the calls persist, notify the police immediately.)
  6. You are baby-sitting, and the parents come home after dark. You rode your bicycle to get there. What should you do about your bike? (Leave it there and pick it up the next day. Ask the mother to take you home.)
  7. Someone you don't know asks you to baby-sit. What should you say? (Before agreeing to baby-sit, counsel with your parent. Have them follow up and find out about the family that asked you.)
  8. You are returning from a walk and you notice that your house's door looks like it has been damaged. What should you do? (Do NOT go into the house. Go immediately to a neighbor's home and telephone the police.)
  9. Someone you do not know pulls his car up to the curb and asks you for directions. What should you tell him? (Move away from him, and from a safe distance direct him to a local business for directions, but watch carefully for any sign of him leaving his car. If he looks like he will be getting out of the vehicle, do NOT stay or answer; run to the nearest safe house immediately.)
- Remind the children that being prepared can keep them safe because they will know how to react under possibly dangerous conditions. Use this time to calm fears through preparation.

Family Ideas

Talk about each safety situation in family home evening. Remind your children that "if ye are prepared ye shall not fear" (D&C 38:30).

Water Safety

Before You Meet

1. Make arrangements with your local pool or Red Cross for your group to receive a presentation on water safety. Specify the ages and size of your group. Request water safety pamphlets for each child.
2. Provide for adequate transportation, if necessary. Fill out any travel permits required by your ward or stake.

Activity

- Take the children to the pool or Red Cross facility.
- Receive the presentation on water safety.
- Send a water safety pamphlet home with each child.

Family Ideas

Read and discuss the water safety pamphlet with your family.

Service
and Citizenship

To help me enjoy serving others in my family, my neighborhood, my ward, and my country.

Singing the National Anthem

Materials Needed

Sheet music, piano.

Before You Meet

1. Arrange for a specialist to teach the group how to sing the national anthem. Request that the group memorize the first verse.
2. Arrange for an accompanist.
3. Be prepared to share historical background information about the national anthem.
4. Note to leader: Consider providing an opportunity for the group to perform the musical number at a later date, such as an achievement days recognition activity.

Activity

- Give a presentation about the history of the national anthem. Include who wrote it and under what circumstances.
- Let the specialist teach the national anthem to the group.

Learning About Disabilities

Materials Needed

Supplies necessary for any chosen activities.

Before You Meet

Before participating in this activity, inquire as to how disabled people in your area prefer to be addressed. Some people prefer terms such as *disabled* or *challenged*. Be especially sensitive to anyone in your area that might be disabled in any way.

Activity

- Briefly explain the purposes of this activity.
- Select two or three of the following activities and have all the children participate in them.

  1. Divide the group into pairs, and have them talk to each other for one or two minutes with a large piece of candy in their mouths. Use a topic of your choice.
  2. Put on a sock and shoe with one hand.
  3. Try to read a sentence by looking at its reflection in a mirror.
  4. Try to stack blocks while blindfolded.
  5. Write your name backwards.
  6. Divide into pairs, and talk about school while wearing earplugs.
  7. Use crutches to walk up a small set of stairs.

- Briefly have the children discuss how they felt as they were experiencing these disabilities. Acknowledge their frustrations, and explain that many people face difficulties like these every day. Help them understand that Heavenly Father loves all his children very much and gives each one blessings and talents.
- Briefly discuss ways that disabled people can be made welcome. Explain that many times disabled people want others to look beyond their disabilities and accept them for who they are.

Family Ideas

Talk with your child about disabled people. If possible, plan an activity that will help her discover the value and friendship that a disabled person has to offer.

Service Coupon Book

Materials Needed

Service coupons (see page 92), pens, scissors, stapler, staples.

Before You Meet

Make copies of the service coupon sheet.

Activity

- Discuss the various types of service that can be offered in our families. Include free baby-sitting, setting the table, sweeping a sidewalk, giving a hug, washing dishes, making a special snack, and so on.
- Give each child a service coupon sheet and have her cut out the individual coupons.
- Help the children fill out the coupons with services they can offer.
- Assemble each child's coupons together to form a small coupon book. Bind it together with staples at the side.
- Encourage the children to go home and give the coupon book to someone special. Remind them to offer the service with a happy attitude.

Family Ideas

Be sure to redeem the coupons and recognize your child's efforts in service.

Service Coupon

Redeem this coupon for the
following service:

_____

From:

Service Coupon

Redeem this coupon for the
following service:

_____

From:

Service Coupon

Redeem this coupon for the
following service:

_____

From:

Service Coupon

Redeem this coupon for the
following service:

_____

From:

Service Coupon

Redeem this coupon for the
following service:

_____

From:

Service Coupon

Redeem this coupon for the
following service:

_____

From:

Service Coupon

Redeem this coupon for the
following service:

_____

From:

Service Coupon

Redeem this coupon for the
following service:

_____

From:

Making a Community Map

Materials Needed

Butcher paper, pencils, markers or crayons.

Before You Meet

1. Draw the main streets in your community on the butcher paper.
2. Optional idea: Give each child a poster board, and have the children make individual maps instead.

Activity

- Have the children fill in the map of their community. Using the streets as guides, draw houses, businesses, libraries, schools, or other buildings. If you have a large group, assign areas.
- Talk about the different places that the children are drawing.
- When the map is finished, have the children find the best route from their homes to other places on the map (for instance, to the library, school, church, and so forth).
- Display the map on recognition night.

Community Cleanup

Materials Needed

Gloves, plastic grocery bags, large trash bags.

Before You Meet

Select a location for your cleanup project. Consider school grounds, church yards, parks, and so on.

Activity

- Make sure each child has a pair of gloves and a plastic grocery sack. (Small bags are easier for the children to handle.)
- As a group, work together to pick up trash and other debris. Empty their sacks into larger trash bags as needed.
- After the area is clean, discuss how nice it looks and compliment the children on their work. Challenge them to always remember to put their litter in a trash barrel.

Family Ideas

Plan a family yard cleanup day to help keep the community beautiful.

Respecting Your Country's Flag

Materials Needed

A flag, thank-you card, envelope, stamp.

Before You Meet

Invite an armed services veteran to speak about honoring the country's flag and to explain what the flag stands for. Give specific time limits and group size.

Activity

- Introduce your guest and allow time for the presentation.
- Give the children the opportunity to ask questions and make comments.
- Demonstrate the correct way to use and treat the flag. Discuss how the correct way shows respect. Give each child the opportunity to handle the flag.
- Let your children sign and mail a thank-you card to your guest following the activity.

Family Ideas

Have a family home evening on being a good citizen.

Spirituality

*To give me opportunities to learn the
gospel, share it with others,
and prepare for temple blessings.*

Making a Temple Picture

Materials Needed

Various colors of heavy parchment-style paper, rubber cement, scissors, rulers, a wallet-sized picture of a temple for each child.

Before You Meet

1. Ask each child to bring a personal wallet-sized photo of herself.
2. Make a temple picture to show the children what it will look like.

Activity

- Choose two colors of parchment-style paper for this project. The foundation (or background) piece will measure 8″ x 10″ and should be a relatively neutral color. The other color will act as an accent and should complement the color of the foundation piece.
- Measure and cut the accent-color paper into rectangles $1/4''$ to $1/2''$ larger than the two pictures.
- Glue the temple picture to one rectangle and the photo to the other.
- Position the two accent rectangles on the foundation paper where you want them, then glue them in place.
- Allow the glue to dry.

Family Ideas

Place the temple picture into an 8″ x 10″ frame and find a place for it in the child's room.

Being a Missionary

Materials Needed

Self-adhesive name tags, simple refreshments, thank-you note, envelope, stamp, pen.

Before You Meet

1. Contact the full-time missionaries or the stake missionaries, and arrange to have them give a presentation to your group suggesting ways they can be missionaries now. Specify the age of your group.
2. Make a missionary badge for each child by writing her name on a name tag and printing "The Church of JESUS CHRIST of Latter-day Saints" at the bottom.
3. Prepare simple refreshments.

Activity

- Give each child her missionary badge as she arrives.
- Welcome and introduce the missionaries.
- Receive their presentation, and allow the children to ask questions and make brief comments.
- Serve refreshments.
- Let your group sign and mail a thank-you card following the activity.

Family Ideas

Invite your child to share ideas during family home evening about how to be a missionary.

Article of Faith Puzzles

Materials Needed

Index cards, glue sticks.

Before You Meet

1. Divide each article of faith into several phrases. Make a copy for every child.
2. Make a complete set for yourself and use them as the children gather for other activities.
3. Note to the leader: You might not want to do all thirteen articles of faith in one activity. Choose to do two or three each quarter or do one during a short activity.

Activity

- Have the children cut out the phrases and glue them onto different index cards. Repeat until the entire article of faith is finished.
- Continue to repeat the process until every article of faith is finished.
- Give children a chance to put their puzzle together by putting the phrases in the correct order.
- Challenge them to use these puzzles to help them learn the articles of faith.

Family Ideas

Use your child's article of faith puzzles in family home evening as an activity.

Prayer Rug

Materials Needed

Carpet sample mats (available at carpet stores), acrylic paint, brushes, letter stencils.

Before You Meet

Arrange for help with this activity. If needed, call a specialist who is familiar with stenciling.

Activity

- Help the children use letter stencils to personalize their carpet squares (for example, "Melissa's Prayer Rug"). Flowers, hearts, or other designs can be added.
- Let the rugs dry thoroughly.
- Instruct the children to take the rugs home and place them next to their beds to remind them to kneel and pray each morning and evening.

Listening to Scripture Stories

Materials Needed

Camera, paper and pens, heavy paper, a manila envelope for each storyteller, plastic sheet protectors for each child.

Before You Meet

1. Contact one or two older individuals in your ward. Explain the goal of introducing the children to stories about spiritual experiences. Ask them to come and retell a favorite story from the scriptures and explain how that story has helped strengthen their faith or testimony. Be specific about time limits.
2. Make arrangements to take pictures of the achievement day children with their special guests.

Activity

- Introduce your guests and turn the time to them.
- Take pictures of the children and their guests.
- After the stories have been shared, have the children write about their experience and what they may have learned.
- Gather the written experiences from the children.

Before the next achievement activity—

- Make a copy of each child's written experience and develop the pictures that were taken.
- Glue or tape a picture onto the heavy paper and place it, along with copies of each child's experience, into the manila envelope.
- If you desire, make additional copies of the pictures for each of the children, glue them to another sheet of paper, and attach the original copy of their experience. Place these inside plastic sheet protectors and give them to the children.
- Use the next activity to deliver the manila envelopes as a thank-you gift to your guests.

Scripture Cards

Materials Needed

Scriptures, index cards, pens, scripture pencils.

Before You Meet

1. Notify each child to bring her scriptures.
2. Prepare a list of five or six short but meaningful scriptures. Make copies of the list for every child.

Activity

- Explain how scripture cards can help acquaint us with the scriptures.
- Show the list to the children and find the first scripture together.
- Read through the scripture, mark it with the scripture pencil, and discuss what it means.
- Have the children place the scripture reference (for instance, "John 13:34") and a brief description ("Love one another") on the card, and place it like a bookmarker to hold the place of that scripture.
- Repeat until the list is completed.
- Challenge the children to look at and familiarize themselves with these scriptures during the coming month.

Family Ideas

Help your child become familiar with the scriptures marked in her book.

A Book of Faith-Promoting Stories

Materials Needed

Two or three copies of the *Friend* magazine for each child, binders, plastic sheet protectors, white paper, scissors.

Before You Meet

1. Collect old issues of the *Friend* magazine from ward members.
2. Ask each child to bring a 1″ or 1 1/2″ three-ring binder.
3. Select a faith-promoting story to read to your group.

Activity

- Read the selected story to your group. Point out to the children that many spiritual stories and articles can strengthen our faith and testimonies. Explain that the purpose of the activity is to start a collection of good stories that they can use for talks, family home evening lessons, or other good purposes.
- Let each child look through and read the articles in the magazines. Have them cut out two or three of their favorites. Remind them to be selective and choose ones that will be meaningful to them.
- Help the children put the articles into sheet protectors. Use plain paper as a backing or put the articles back to back.
- Assemble the sheets in the binders.

Family Ideas

Invite your child to share one of her stories during family home evening. Encourage her to continue to add stories to her book.

Sports and
Physical Fitness

*To help me learn how to keep my body
strong through physical activities.*

Basketball Skills

Materials Needed

Several basketballs, hazard cones or other markers for an obstacle course.

Before You Meet

1. Ask your ward Young Women's basketball team and their coach to present this activity. Explain that the purpose of this activity is for the children to learn how to handle the basketball. Suggest the ideas found in this activity section or others of their choosing.
2. Make arrangements for the use of a basketball court.
3. Follow up this activity with "Attending a Basketball Game" (see page 113).

Activity

- Welcome the Young Women's basketball team and their coach.
- Give each girl a basketball and have her dribble or bounce it. As they are able, practice the following variations: right-hand dribbling, left-hand dribbling, and dribbling using alternating right and left hands.
- Teach the children to dribble the ball as they walk the length of the basketball court. Divide the children into two groups and conduct a relay using this skill.
- Place hazard cones in a straight line. Teach the children how to weave back and forth through the line of cones as they dribble the ball.
- Divide the children into two groups. Have them form two straight lines facing each other. Pair up the children across from each other, and have them practice passing the ball back and forth.

  Chest pass: Hold the ball chest high and, using both hands, pass straight across to a partner.
  Overhead pass: Hold the ball overhead with both hands and pass to a partner.
  Bounce pass: Pass the ball by bouncing it on the floor one time between partners.
  Alternating passes: Start the ball at the beginning of the two lines. Let the girls choose how they want to pass the ball to the person in front of them. Pass in a zigzag manner between children, as the ball works its way to the end of the lines. Repeat as time allows.

Family Ideas

Let your child demonstrate the various dribbling and passing skills she has learned. Practice with her as she tries to develop these skills.

Frisbee® Golf

Materials Needed

Nine hula hoops, a Frisbee® for every child.

Before You Meet

1. Make whatever arrangements are necessary to reserve a large grassy area for your group.
2. Set up the Frisbee® golf course. The hula hoops will be considered the holes. If you desire you can use a wooden pole to mark each hole.
3. Make a list with every child's name on it.
4. For safety, have the children move away from the hole as they complete that section.

Activity

- Give each child a Frisbee®. Explain that the objective of the game is to get the Frisbee® into the hula hoops.
- Have the children take turns throwing their Frisbees® toward the first hole. After everyone has had a chance, have the children stand beside their Frisbees®.
- Let the child closest to the first hula hoop throw her Frisbee® until she makes it in the hole. Repeat until every child has had the opportunity. No child can make more than four throws.

Bike Ride and Picnic

Materials Needed

A bicycle, helmet, sack lunch, and bicycle safety pamphlet for each child. (Pamphlets are usually available through your local law enforcement agency.)

Before You Meet

1. Select an appropriate route and distance for your group to bicycle. Plan for a picnic area about midway.
2. Make arrangements for sack lunches to be at the designated picnic area.
3. Read the pamphlet and be prepared to give instructions on bicycle safety.

Activity

-   Discuss bicycle safety rules with the group.
-   Ride in a single-file line along your predetermined route.
-   Stop at the picnic area for lunch.
-   Complete your bike ride.
-   Give each child a bicycle safety pamphlet to take home.

Family Ideas

Read and discuss the bicycle safety pamphlet with your child.

Water Activity

Materials Needed

Any materials necessary for the chosen activities.

Before You Meet

1. Decide on the number and types of water games you will use.
2. Contact the children and advise them to bring a towel and come dressed to get wet.

Activity

Use two or more of the following activities.

Sponge Baseball: Divide the children into two teams and play a one-inning game of baseball. Give the pitcher a bucket of water that contains several sponges. Instead of using a regular baseball, use sponges. Be sure to resoak the sponges after every pitch or hit. (Alternative suggestion: Give each child the opportunity to hit the sponge with a bat. The longest hit wins.)

Running the Gauntlet: Ask for a volunteer or choose someone to be It. Have everyone else form two lines about eight to ten feet apart. Give each child a paper cup filled with water. The children try to throw their water on It as she runs between the two lines. The fun begins as the children, trying to throw their water on It, also hit the opposite line.

Water Balloon Toss: Divide the children into pairs and give each pair a water balloon. Toss the balloon back and forth, each time taking a step backward. The winner is the last one to catch an unbroken balloon. Play several times, and then allow the winners to play each other until one champion team is left.

Water Balloon Volleyball: Give each pair of children a bath towel. Divide the pairs into two teams. Each pair uses their towels to catch and return the balloons back to the other team.

Swimming Pool Kickball: Place a small swimming pool at first, second, and third bases. Fill each swimming pool with water. Play kickball as usual, but the kicker must put her foot into the pool to be safe on the base.

Water Tag: Give each child a cup of water. Everyone uses their water to tag the other people. A tag is a water hit on any part of the torso. Cups can be refilled as often as necessary by those who have not yet been tagged. The last untagged person is the winner. Provide a large bucket or container of water to refill cups.

Attending a Basketball Game

Before You Meet

1. Make arrangements for your group to attend a Young Women's basketball game. Visit with the coach and explain that the purpose is for the children to observe good basketball skills and good sportsmanship.
2. This activity is most effective following the "Basketball Skills" activity (see page 109).

Activity

Attend the basketball game as a group. Encourage the girls to watch the passing and dribbling skills that the players use.

Family Ideas

Attend a basketball game or other sporting event together as a family. Discuss the skills that the athletes have developed.

Pioneer Game Time

Materials Needed

Any materials necessary for selected activities.

Before You Meet

Select two or three of the games provided below or use others of your own choosing.

Activity

- Explain to the children that pioneer children didn't have many of the organized sports that we do today.
- Play each selected game.

  Duck, Duck, Goose: All players sit in a circle, except the player who is It. She walks around the outside of the circle and touches each other player's head, saying "duck." After calling out "duck" a few times, It touches a head and says "goose." The player who is the goose has to jump up and chase It around the circle. If It runs around the circle and sits in goose's spot without being tagged, the goose becomes It.

  Gunnysack Relay: Have the children form a line. Give the first child a gunny-sack. The child should step inside the sack and hold the sides up. She is to jump with both feet together towards the finish line. When she reaches the end of the relay course, she steps out of the bag, runs back to the line, and gives the sack to the next child. Continue until all the children have had a turn.

  Ringtaw: Draw a large circle on the ground and a smaller circle inside of it. Place several small marbles, called "nibs," in the small circle. From the outside of the large circle, the players take turns flicking a large marble, called a "shooter," into the circles. The goal is to knock the nibs out of the circles.

  Jackstraws: To play, you must have a pile of wood splinters that are heaped in the middle of a hard surface. Each player has a turn removing one stick from the pile. The challenge is to do so without moving any of the other sticks. A suggestion for jackstraws might be Pick-up Sticks or skewer sticks.

  Ringtoss: Cut stiff rope in 20″ lengths. Shape them into circles and secure the ends with heavy tape. Drive stakes into the ground, leaving about eight to ten inches above ground. Determine the appropriate tossing distance for your group of children, and mark a line for them to stand behind as they toss the rings. The objective is for the children to toss the rope rings over the stakes. An indoor variation of this can be done by using cans of soup in place of stakes.

  Tiddlywinks: Use chalk or masking tape to "draw" a circle on a hard surface. Place a cup in the center of that circle. Players use a flat disk, called a shooter, to flip other disks, called winks, into that cup. The object is to be the first player to get all of his or her winks in the cup. In a timed game, the winner is the player who gets the most number of winks in the cup.

  Three-legged Race: Mark off a course of about 30 yards. Pair up the children. Tie one person's right leg to her partner's left leg. Have the teams race to the finish line. The first one to cross the finish line is declared the winner.

Achievement Day Calendar

For the Month of _____

Date _____ Time _____ Place _____

- Achievement area and purpose

  _____

  _____

- Special needs or items to bring

  _____

  _____

- Family ideas

  _____

  _____

Date _____ Time _____ Place _____

- Achievement area and purpose

  _____

  _____

- Special needs or items to bring

  _____

  _____

- Family ideas

  _____

  _____

Achievement Day Calendar

For the Month of July

Date ___12___ Time _9:00 a.m._ Place _the ward_

- Achievement area and purpose
  outdoor fun & skills
  build a bird feeder & learn an outdoor game

- Special needs or items to bring
  will have material you need

- Family ideas
  Help your child find a place to hang their bird feeder

Date ___26___ Time _5:30 p.m._ Place _Jefferson Park_

- Achievement area and purpose
  outdoor fun & skills
  building a campfire, having a cookout

- Special needs or items to bring
  bring parents

- Family ideas
  Your child is learning to build a campfire. Have them help you
  next time you go camping.

Presented to

for completing achievements

in the area of:

_____   _____

Achievement Day Leader   *Primary President*

Recognition Certificate

Presented to

_____

for completing achievements

in the area of:

_____

Achievement Day Leader

Primary President

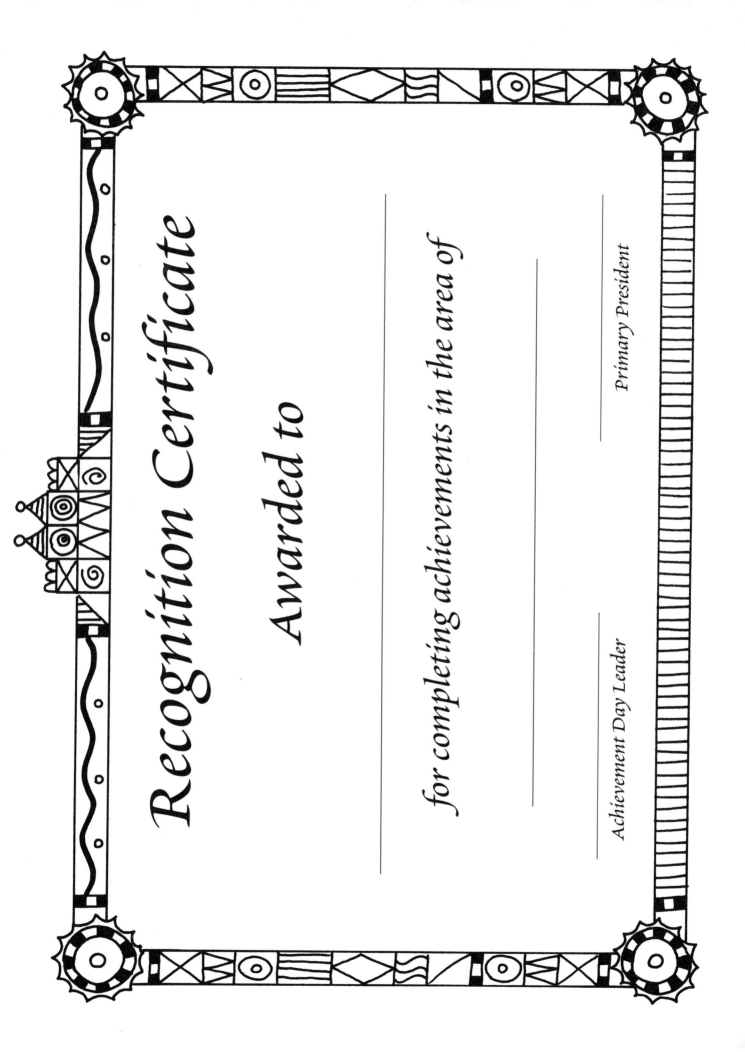

Recognition Certificate

Awarded to

for completing achievements in the area of

_____

Achievement Day Leader

Primary President